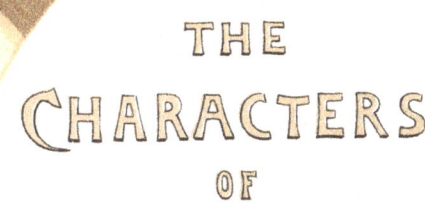

THE CHARACTERS OF CHARLES DICKENS

POURTRAYED IN A SERIES

OF ORIGINAL WATER COLOUR

SKETCHES BY "KYD"

THE CHARACTERS OF CHARLES DICKENS ARE SOMETHING MORE THAN MERE FICTIONAL CREATIONS, MERE CREATURES OF THE IMAGINATION; THEY BREATHE AND LIVE IN REAL FLESH AND BLOOD, THEY EXIST IN OUR VERY MIDST. WE KNOW, OR SEEM TO HAVE KNOWN THEM PERSONALLY; WE HAVE SMILED WITH SAM WELLER, WE HAVE SYMPATHIZED WITH TINY TIM, WE HAVE WEPT WITH LITTLE NELL.   THEY WILL CEASE TO CHARM US ONLY WHEN THE ENGLISH LANGUAGE IS FORGOTTEN, OR HUMAN NATURE CEASES TO EXIST.

RAPHAEL TUCK & SONS,
LONDON, PARIS & NEW YORK.

Printed at the Fine Art Works in London.

Originally Published in 1889 By Raphael Tuck & Son
London, Paris and New York

Reprint ISBN 978-1-58218-901-7
River Moor Books
Scituate Massachusetts 2019

Character Sketches From Charles Dickens
Pourtrayed By Kid

MR. WELLER, SENIOR.

" If ever you're attacked with the gout, sir, jist you marry a widder as, has got a good woice, with a decent notion of usin' it, and you'll never have the gout agin."

PICKWICK PAPERS,—Chapter XX.

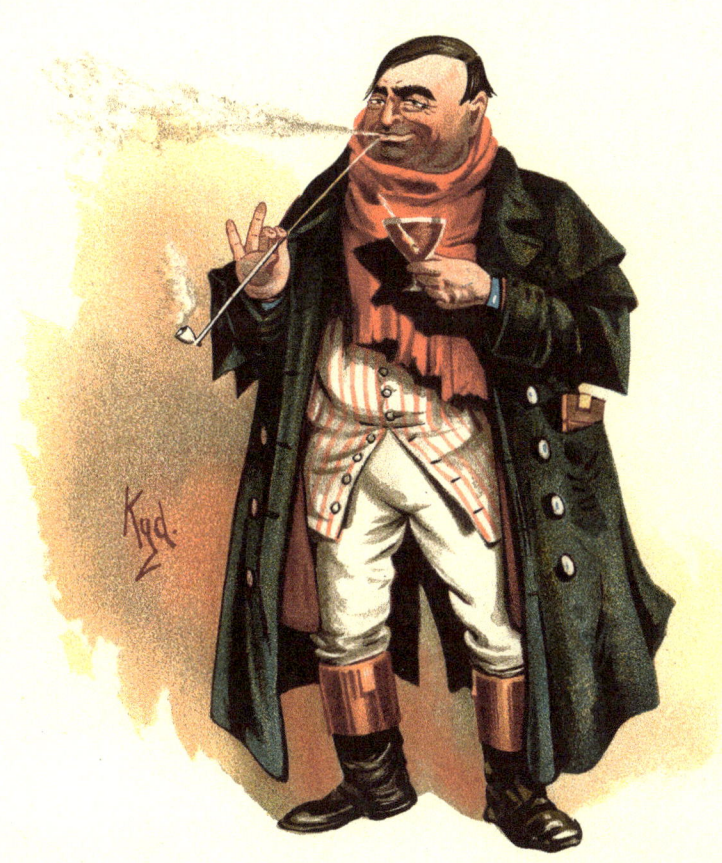

MR WELLER SENIOR

CAPTAIN CUTTLE.

* * * * had been a pilot, or a skipper, or a privateer's-man, or all three perhaps; and was a very salt looking man indeed.

DOMBEY AND SON.- Chapter IV.

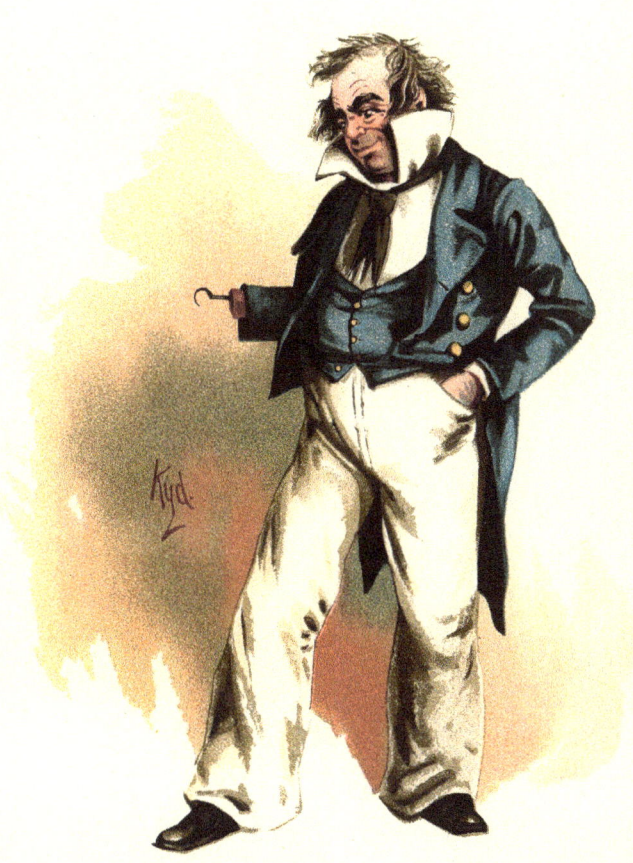

CAPT. CUTTLE.

[DOMBEY & SON.]

MR. STIGGINS.

* * * *walking softly across the room to a well-remembered shelf in one corner, took down a tumbler, and, with great deliberation, put four lumps of sugar in it. Having got thus far, he looked about him again, and sighed grievously.*

PICKWICK PAPERS.—Chapter LII.

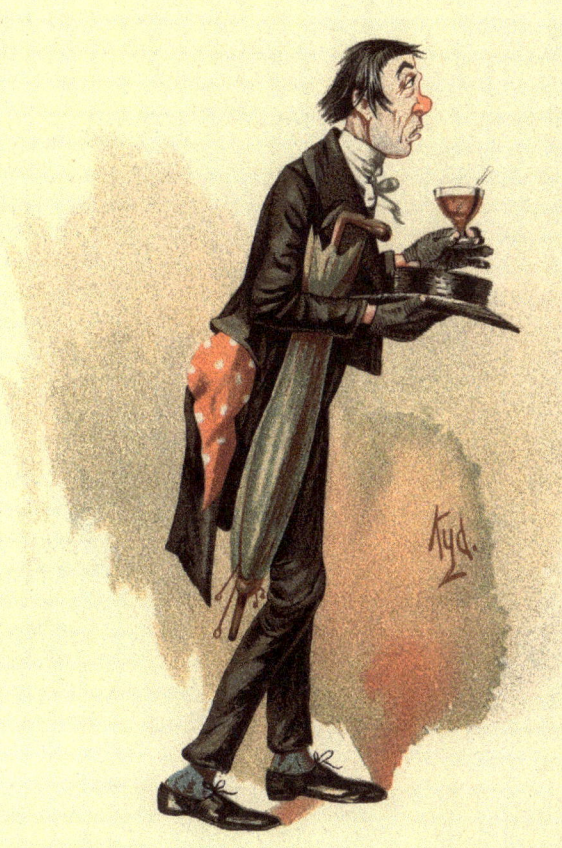

DICK SWIVELLER.

" A select convivial circle called the Glorious Apollers, of which I have the honour to be Perpetual Grand. "

OLD CURIOSITY SHOP.—Chapter XIII.

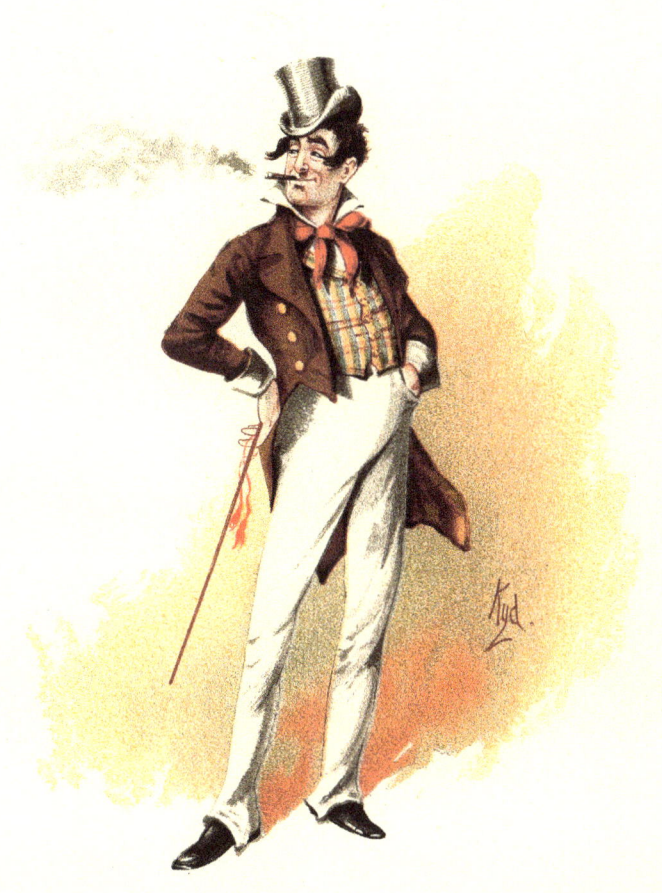

DICK SWIVELLER.

QUILP.

" There's no such thing to be had here," cried the dwarf. "Water for lawyers! Melted lead and brimstone, you mean, nice hot blistering pitch and tar—that's the thing for them."

OLD CURIOSITY SHOP.—Chapter LXII.

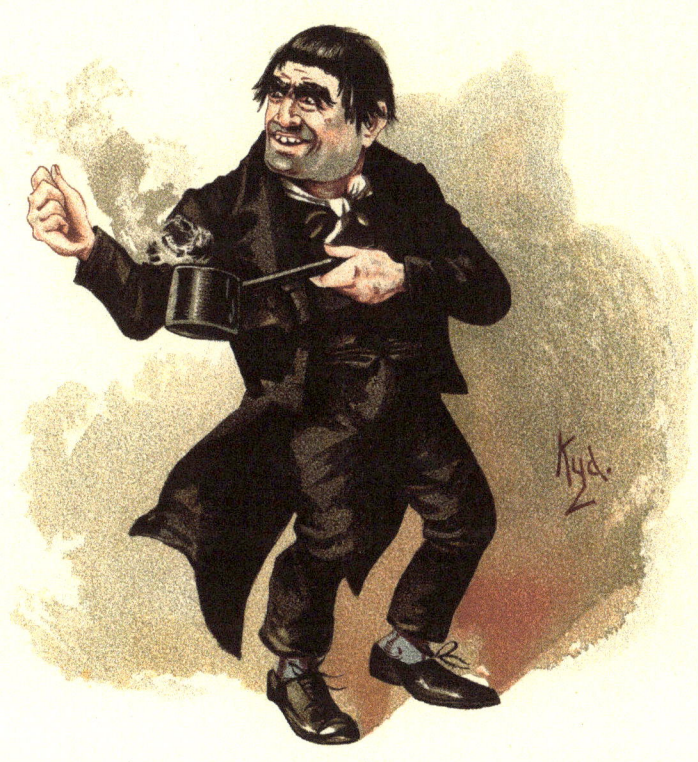

QUILP

THE MARCHIONESS.

" But, please, will you leave a card or message ? "

OLD CURIOSITY SHOP.—Chapter LI.

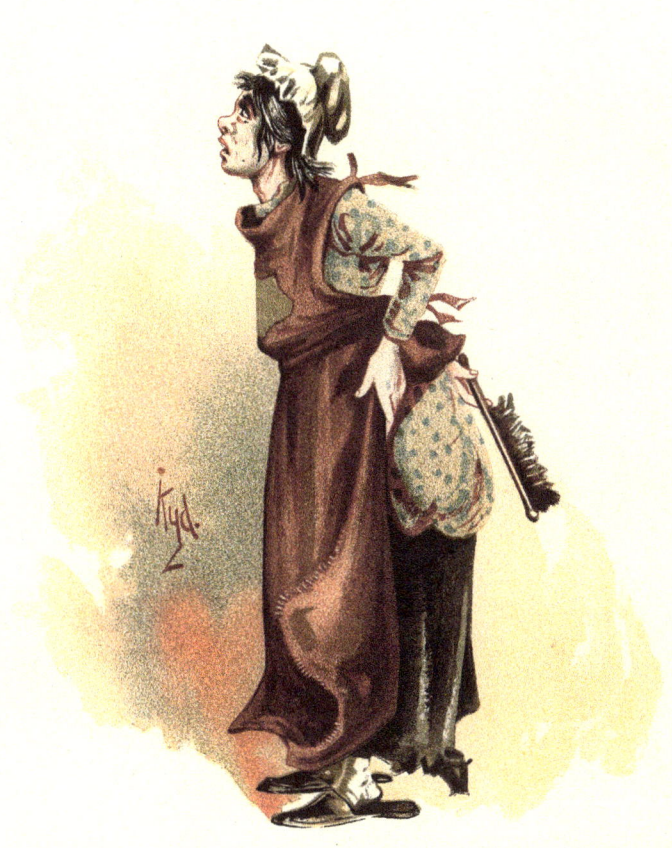

THE LITTLE MARCHIONESS

[OLD CURIOSITY SHOP]

SAMPSON BRASS.

He had a cringing manner, but a very harsh voice; and his blandest smiles were so extremely forbidding, that to have had his company under the least repulsive circumstances, one would have wished him to be out of temper that he might only scowl.

OLD CURIOSITY SHOP.—Chapter XI.

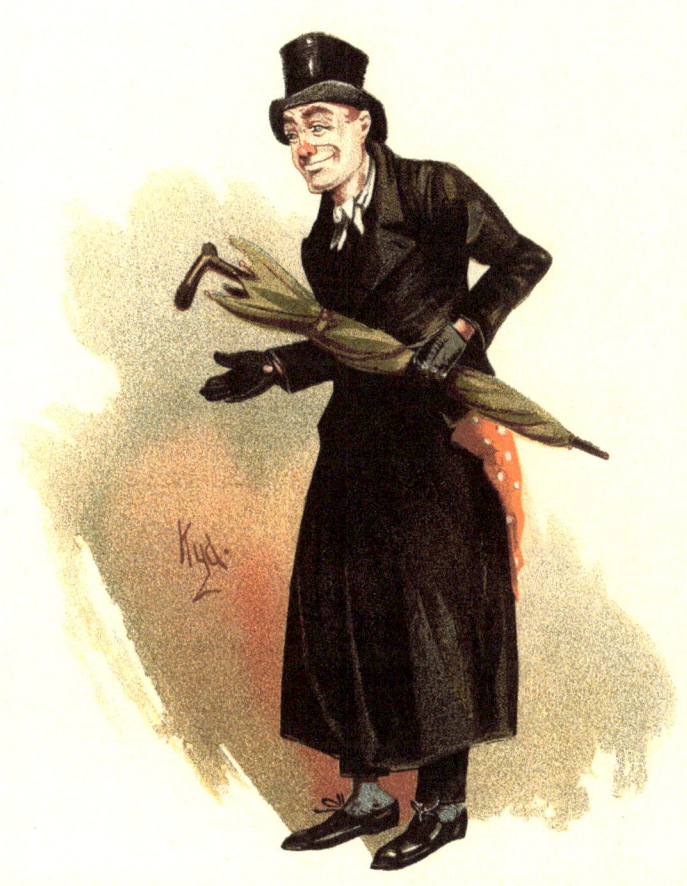

SAMPSON BRASS

OLD CURIOSITY SHOP

MR. PEGGOTTY.

" I'm a-going to seek my niece through the wureld. I'm a-going to find my poor niece in her shame, and bring her back."

DAVID COPPERFIELD.—Chapter XXXI.

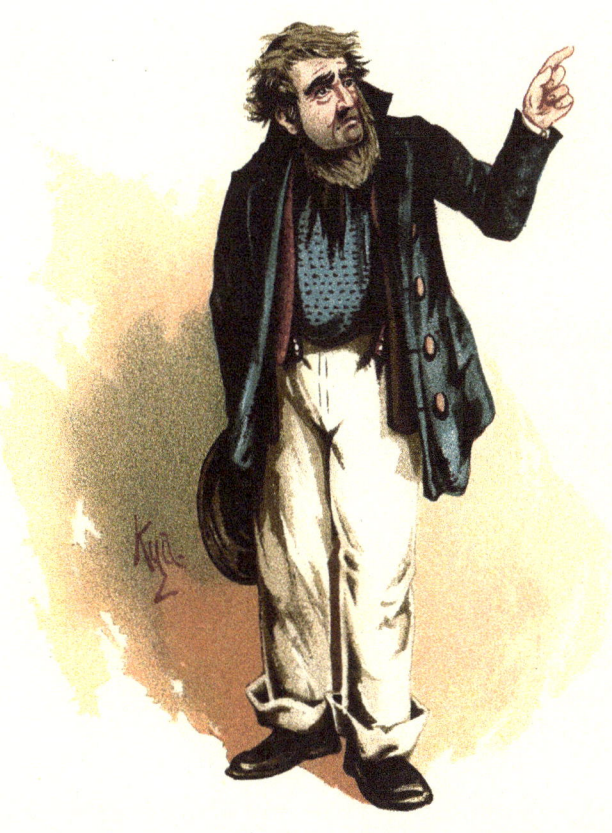

MR PEGGOTTY. [DAVID COPPERFIELD.]

SERGT. BUZFUZ.

" Damages, gentlemen—heavy damages is the only punishment with which you can visit him; the only recompense you can award my client."

PICKWICK PAPERS.—Chapter XXXIV.

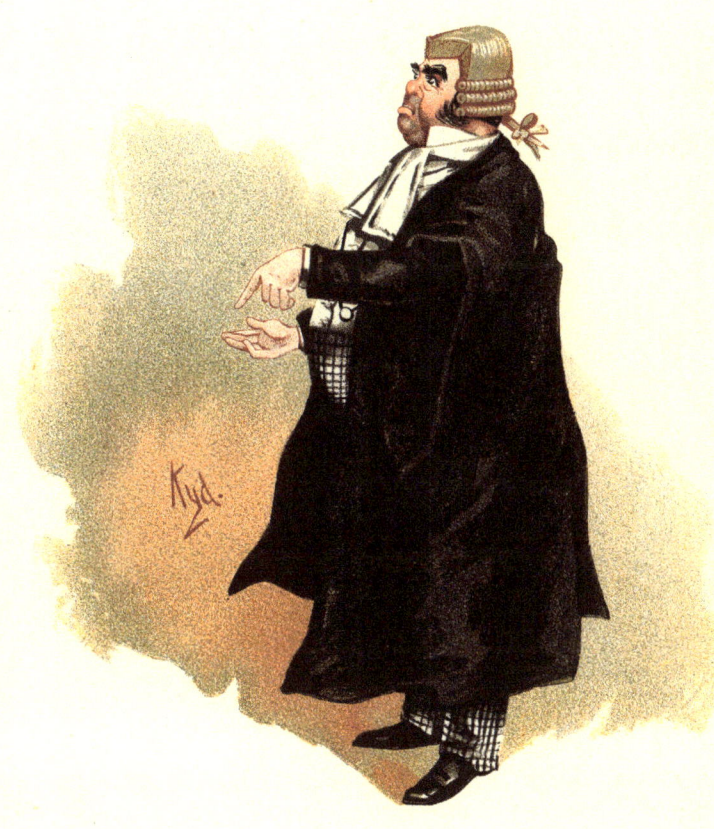

SERJT BUZFUZ.

PICKWICK PAPERS.

SAIREY GAMP.

The face of Mrs. Gamp—the nose in particular—was somewhat red and swollen, and it was difficult to enjoy her society without becoming conscious of a smell of spirits.

MARTIN CHUZZLEWIT.-Chapter XIX.

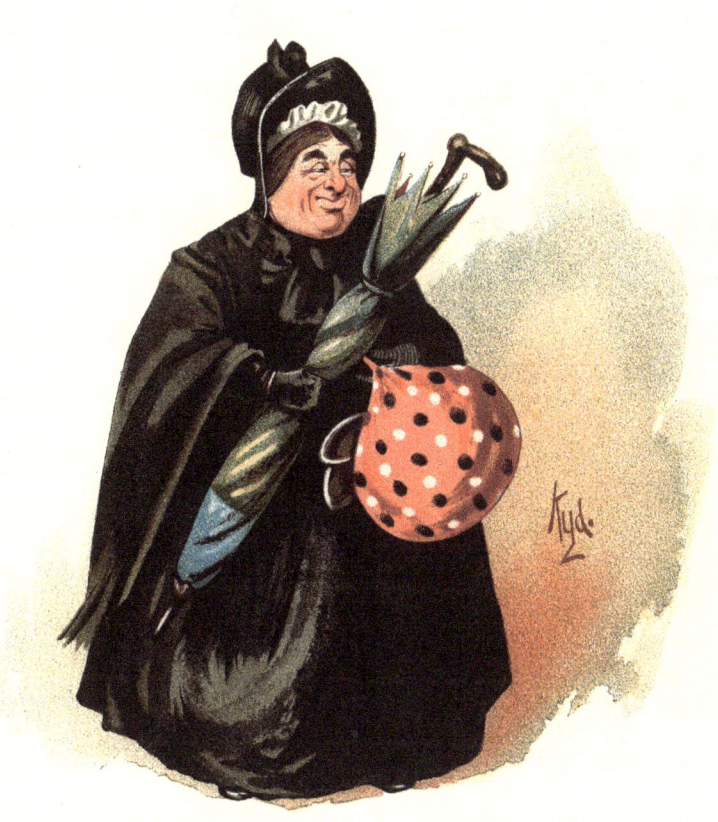

MRS GAMP

MR PICKWICK.

Mr. Pickwick was the personation of kindness and humanity.

PICKWICK PAPERS.—Chapter V.

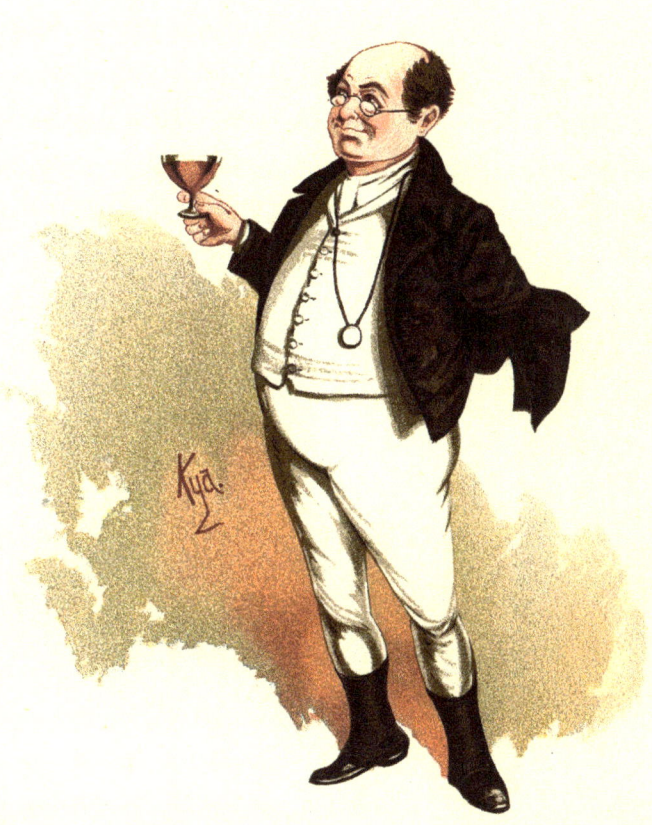

MR PICKWICK.

[PICKWICK PAPERS.]

THE FAT BOY.

" * * # * he's gone to sleep again. Be good enough to pinch him, sir—in the leg, if you please; nothing else wakes him."

PICKWICK PAPERS.—Chapter IV.

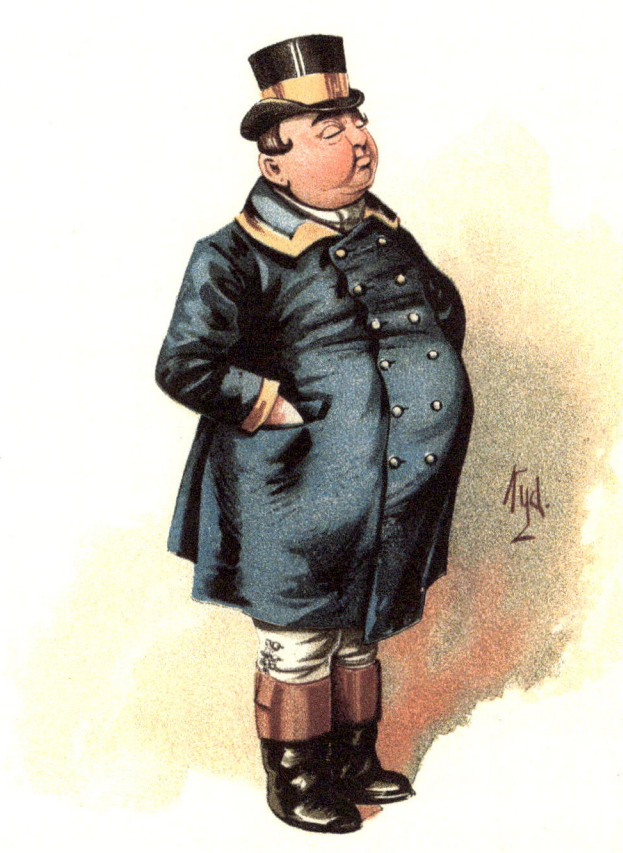

THE FAT BOY

MRS. BARDELL.

Mrs. Bardell could only reply by a look. She had long worshipped Mr. Pickwick at a distance, but here she was, all at once, raised to a pinnacle to which her wildest and most extravagant hopes had never dared to aspire.

PICKWICK PAPERS.—Chapter XII.

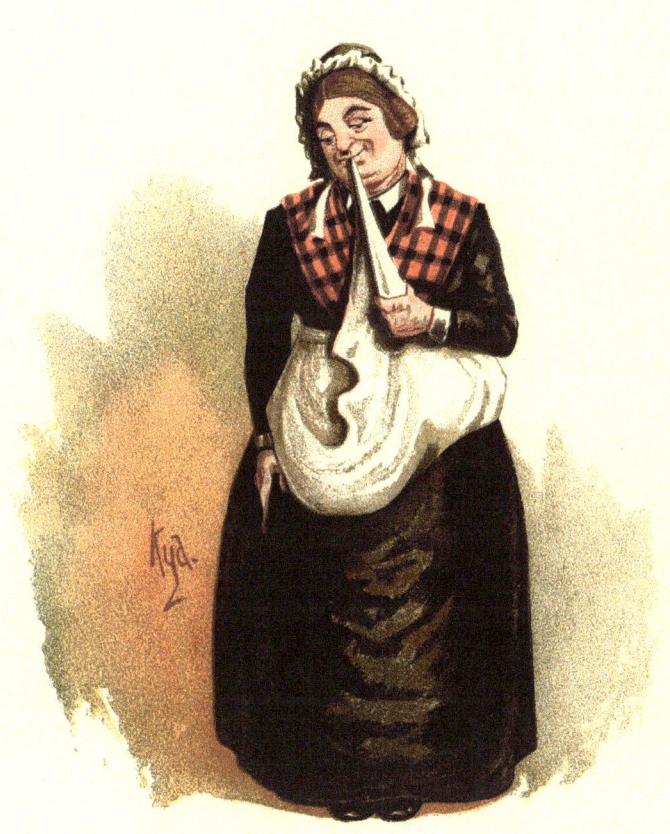

BILL SIKES.

"Well, then, keep quiet," rejoined Sikes, with a growl like that he was accustomed to use when addressing his dog,-"or I'll quiet you for a good long time to come."

OLIVER TWIST.—Chapter XVI.

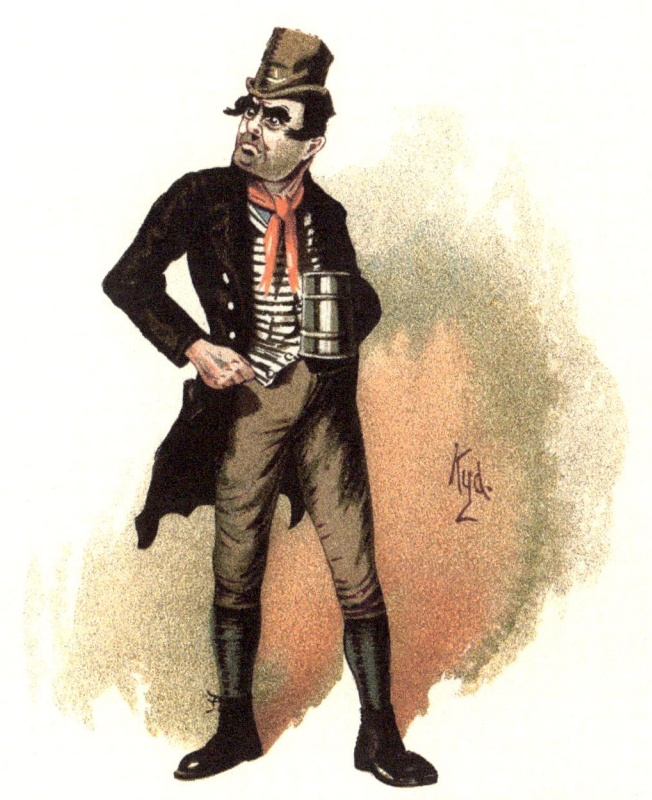

BILL SIKES.

SAM WELLER.

"We eats our biled mutton without capers, and don't care, for horse-radish wen ve can get beef."

PICKWICK PAPERS.—Chapter X.

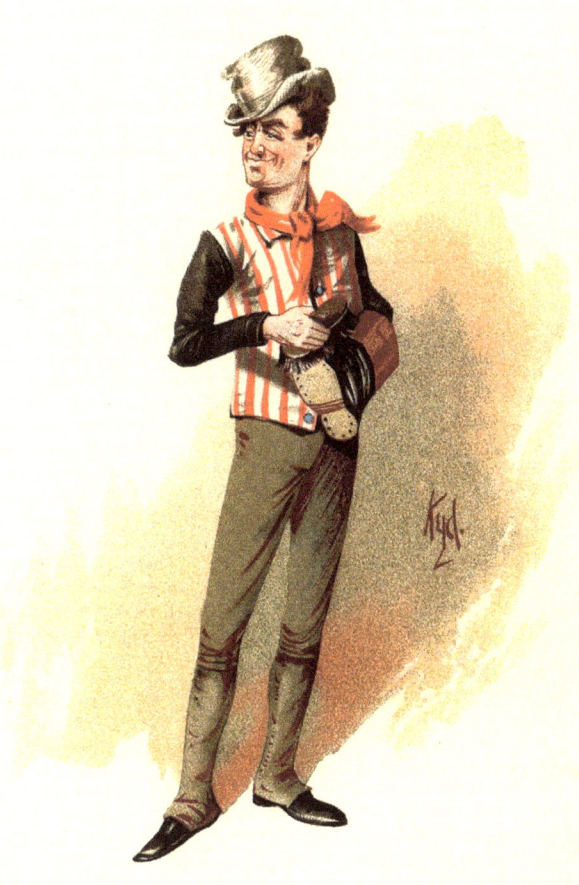

SAM WELLER.

MR. PECKSNIFF.

*" There is no deception, ladies and gentlemen, all
is peace, holy calm pervades me."*

MARTIN CHUZZLEWIT.—Chapter II.

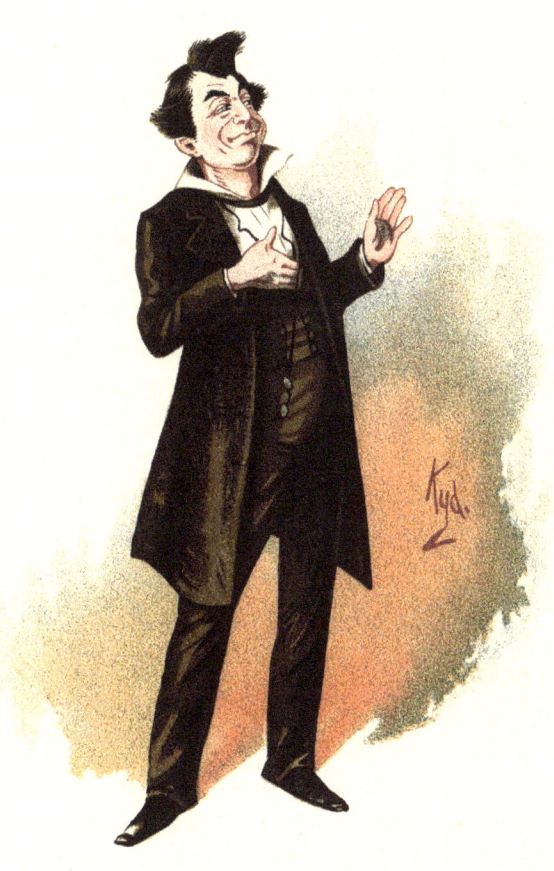

MR PECKSNIFF.   [MARTIN CHUZZLEWIT.]

TOOTS.

" It's of no consequence, thankee."

DOMBEY AND SON,-Chapter XXII.

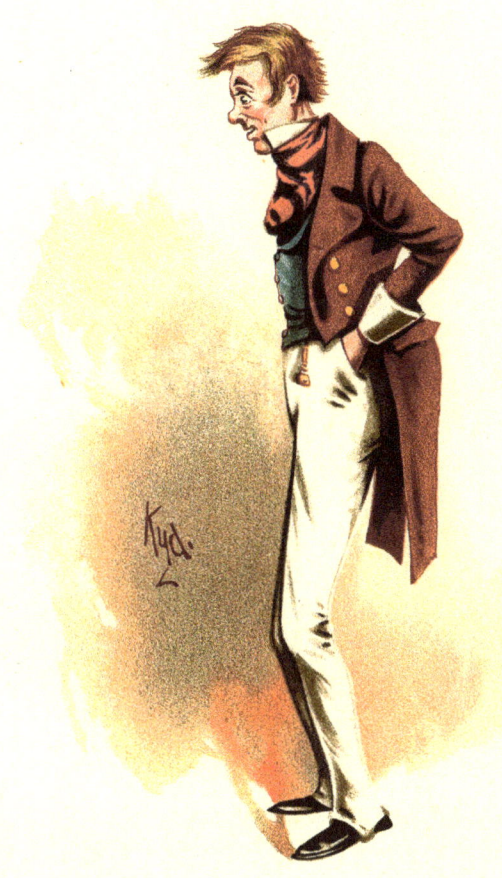

TOOTS

URIAH HEEP.

" *I am well aware that I am the 'umblest person going, let the other be where he may. My mother is likewise a very 'umble person. We live in a numble abode, Master Copperfield, but have much to be thankful for.*"

DAVID COPPERFIELD.—Chapter XVI.

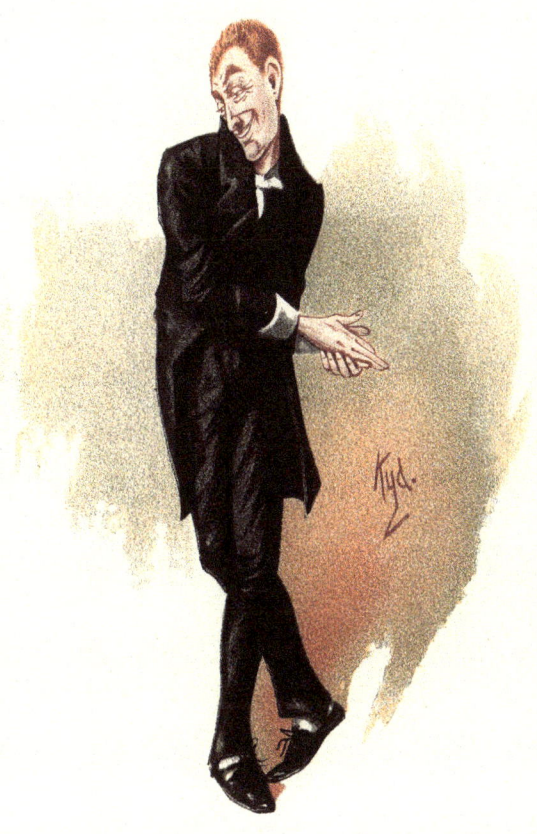

URIAH HEEP.

MR. BUMBLE.

"Do you know this here voice, Oliver? Ain't you afraid of it, sir? Ain't you a trembling while I speak, sir?"

OLIVER TWIST.—Chapter VII.

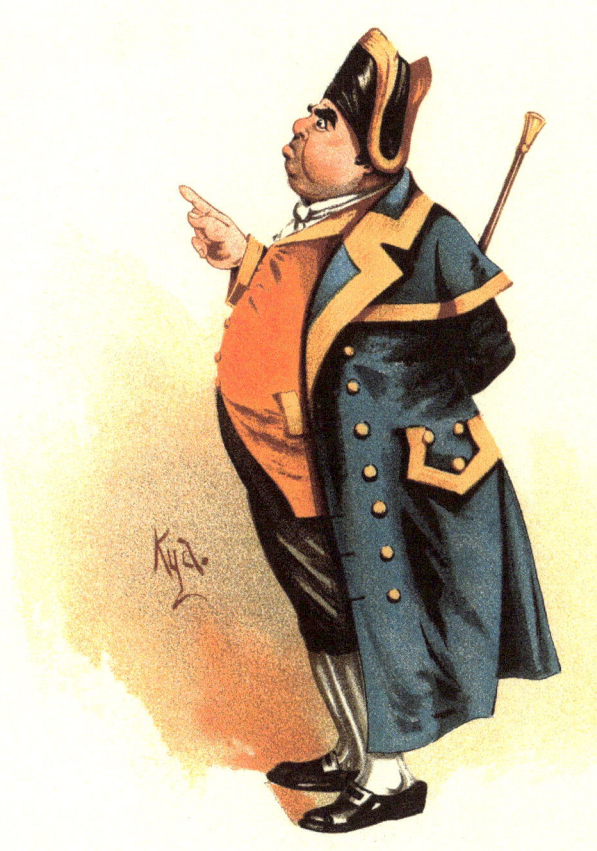

MR BUMBLE. [OLIVER TWIST]

MR. MICAWBER.

* * * # *with a certain condescending- roll in his voice, and a certain indescribable air of doing something genteel.*

DAVID COPPERFIELD.—Chapter XI.

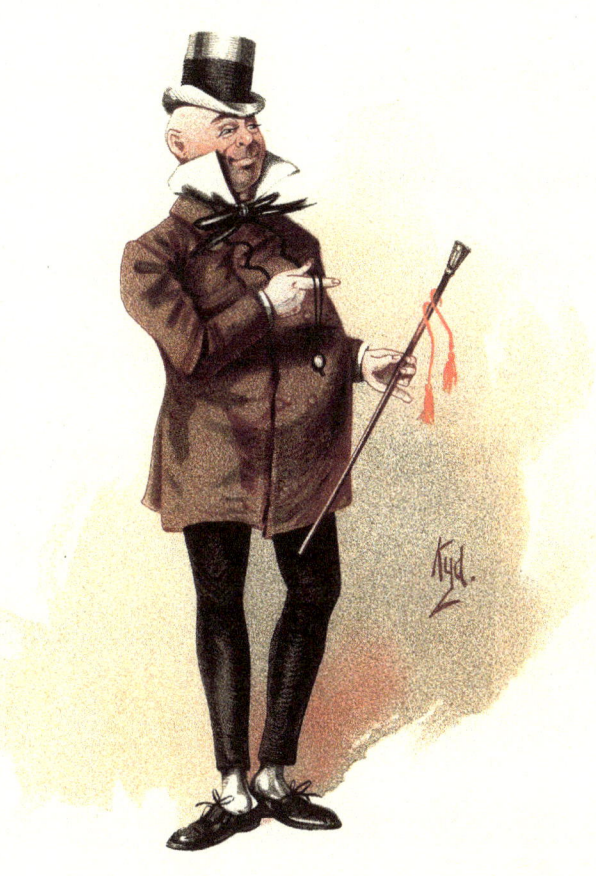

MR MICAWBER.

MR. JINGLE.

"Jingle" said that versatile gentleman, taking the hint at once, 'Jingle—Alfred Jingle, Esq., of No Hall, Nowhere."

PICKWICK PAPERS.—Chapter VII.

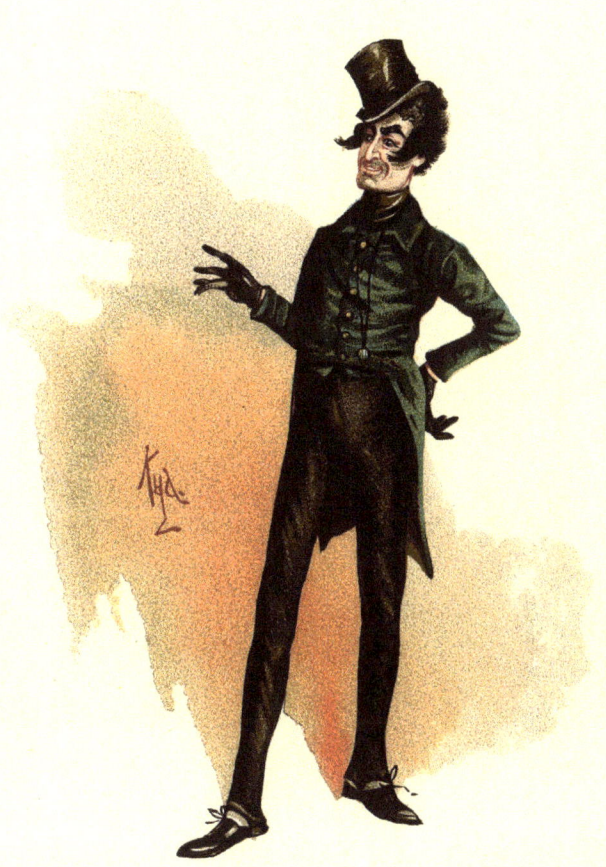

MR ALFRED JINGLE.

MR. WHACKFORD SQUEERS.

*Mr. Squeers had but one eye, and the popular prejudice runs in favour of two, * * # * and when he smiled, his expression bordered closely on the villainous.*

NICHOLAS NICKLEBY.—Chapter IV.

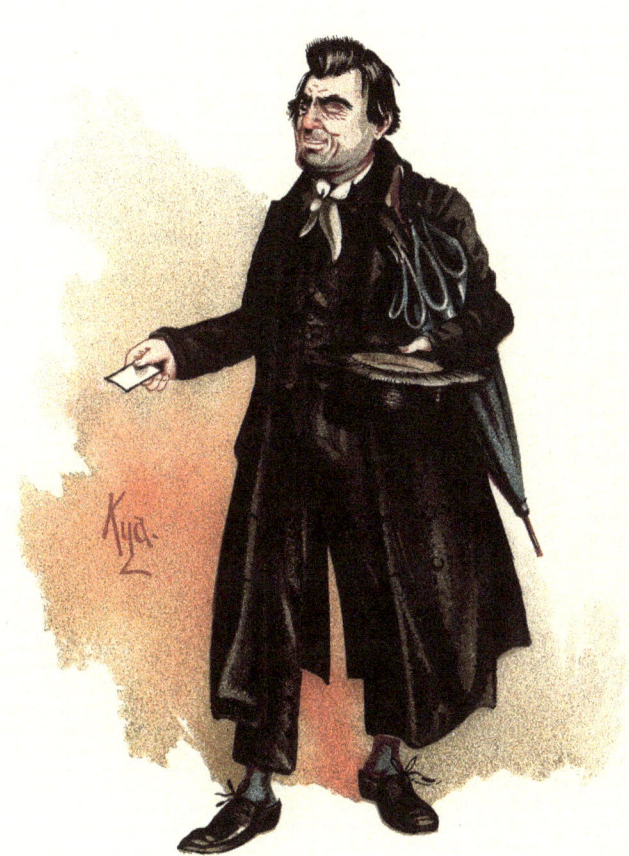

MR. WHACKFORD SQUEERS.

THE ARTFUL DODGER.

* * * # *happened to entertain a violent and deeply-rooted antipathy to going near a police-office on any ground or pretext whatever.*

OLIVER TWIST.—Chapter XIII.

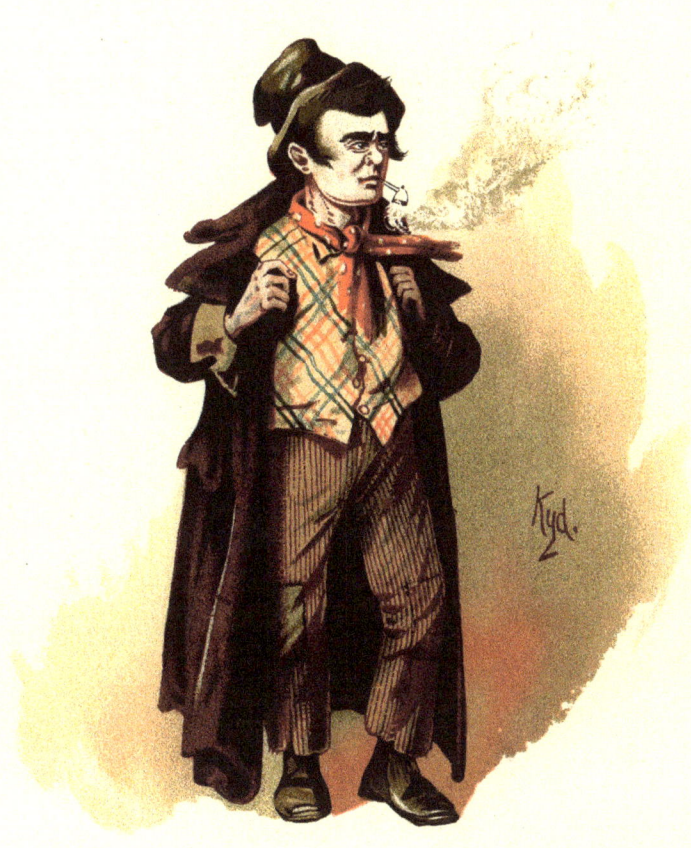

THE ARTFUL DODGER.

[OLIVER TWIST]

TROTTY VECK.

I italic * * * *he had perfect faith-not often tested—in his being able to carry anything that man could lift.*

THE CHIMES.—First Quarter.

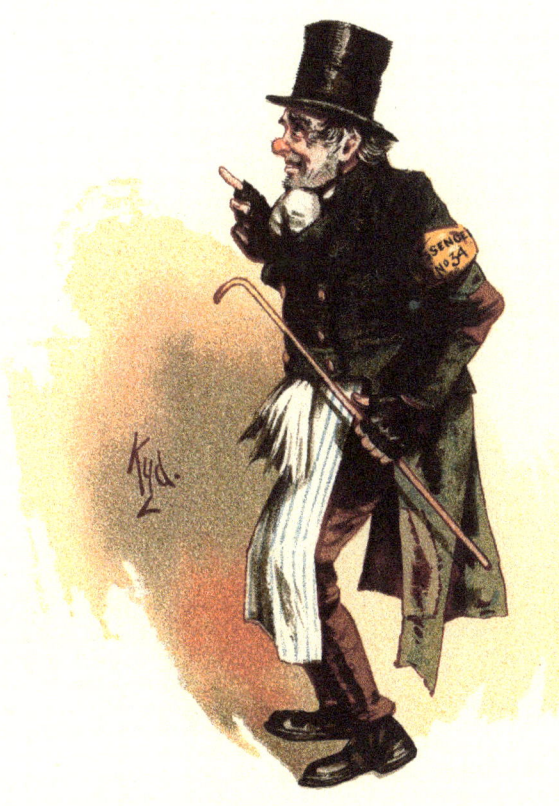

TROTTY VECK.

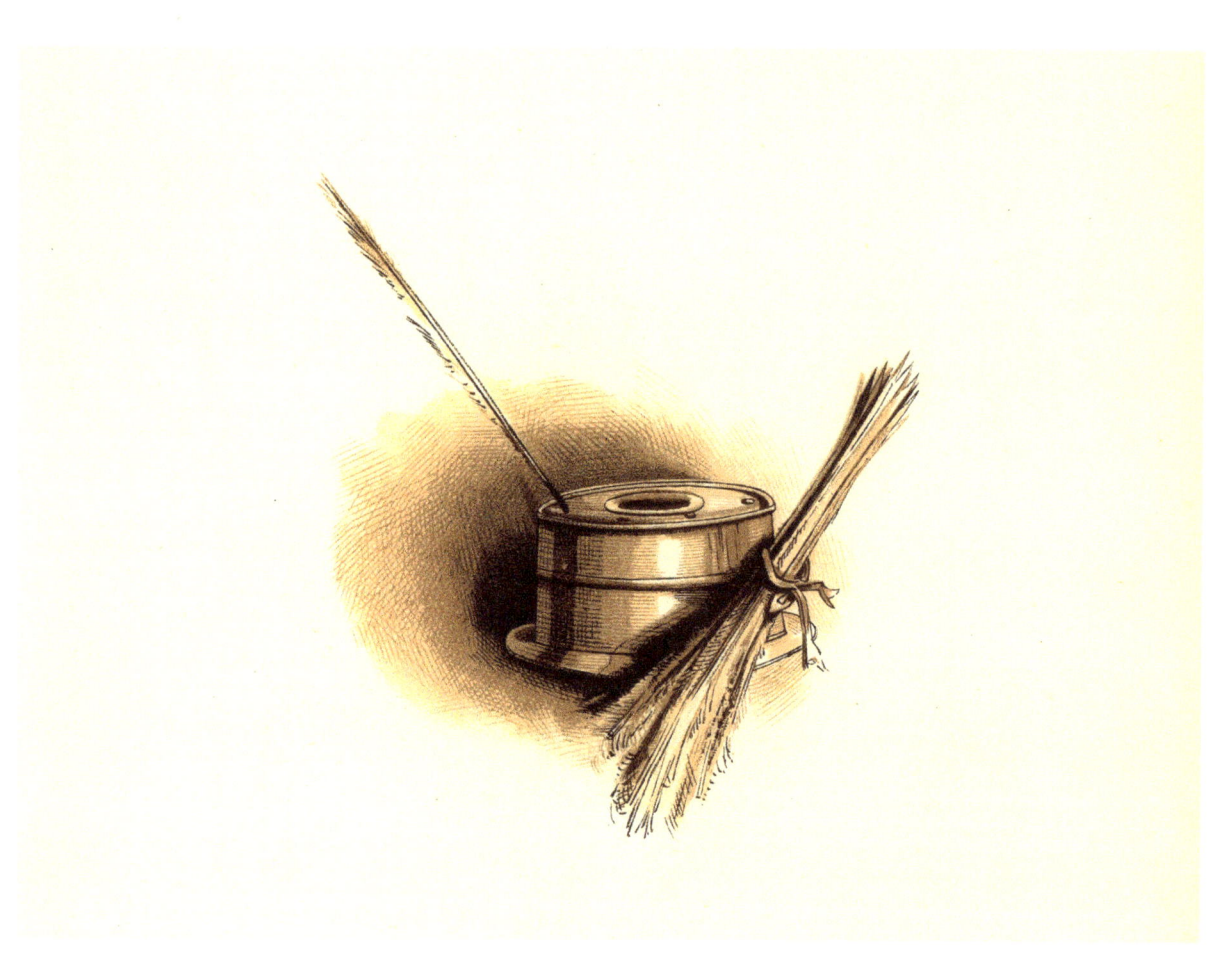

www.ingramcontent.com/pod-product-compliance
Lightning Source LLC
Chambersburg PA
CBHW052137170526
45162CB00004B/42